Editors' Preface to Macmillan Studies in Economics

The rapid growth of academic literature in the field of economics has posed serious problems for both students and teachers of the subject. The latter find it difficult to keep pace with more than a few areas of their subject, so that an inevitable trend towards specialism emerges. The student quickly loses perspective as the maze of theories and models grows and the discipline accommodates an increasing amount of quantitative techniques.

'Macmillan Studies in Economics' is a new series which sets out to provide the student with short, reasonably critical surveys of the developments within the various specialist areas of theoretical and applied economics. At the same time, the studies aim to form an integrated series so that, seen as a whole, they supply a balanced overview of the subject of economics. The emphasis in each study is upon recent work, but each topic will generally be placed in a historical context so that the reader may see the logical development of thought through time. Selected bibliographies are provided to guide readers to more extensive works. Each study aims at a brief treatment of the salient problems in order to avoid clouding the issues in detailed argument. None the less, the texts are largely self-contained, and presume only that the student has some knowledge of elementary microeconomics and macroeconomics.

Mathematical exposition has been adopted only where necessary. Some recent developments in economics are not readily comprehensible without some mathematics and statistics, and quantitative approaches also serve to shorten what would otherwise be lengthy and involved arguments. Where authors have found it necessary to introduce mathematical techniques, these techniques have been kept to a minimum. The emphasis is upon the economics, and not upon the quantitative methods. Later studies in the series will provide analyses of the links between quantitative methods, in particular econometrics, and economic analysis.

MACMILLAN STUDIES IN ECONOMICS

General Editors: D. C. ROWAN and G. R. FISHER

Executive Editor: D. W. PEARCE

Published

John Burton: WAGE INFLATION
Miles Fleming: MONETARY THEORY
C. J. Hawkins: THEORY OF THE FIRM
C. J. Hawkins and D. W. Pearce: CAPITAL INVESTMENT APPRAISAL
David F. Heathfield: PRODUCTION FUNCTIONS
Dudley Jackson: POVERTY
P. N. Junankar: INVESTMENT: THEORIES AND EVIDENCE
J. E. King: LABOUR ECONOMICS
J. A. Kregel: THE THEORY OF ECONOMIC GROWTH
George McKenzie: THE MONETARY THEORY OF INTERNATIONAL TRADE
S. K. Nath: A PERSPECTIVE OF WELFARE ECONOMICS
Antony Peaker: ECONOMIC GROWTH IN MODERN BRITAIN
D. W. Pearce: COST-BENEFIT ANALYSIS
Maurice Peston: PUBLIC GOODS AND THE PUBLIC SECTOR
David Robertson: INTERNATIONAL TRADE POLICY
Charles K. Rowley: ANTITRUST AND ECONOMIC EFFICIENCY
C. H. Sharp: TRANSPORT ECONOMICS
G. K. Shaw: FISCAL POLICY
R. Shone: THE PURE THEORY OF INTERNATIONAL TRADE
Frank J. B. Stilwell: REGIONAL ECONOMIC POLICY
John Vaizey: THE ECONOMICS OF EDUCATION
Peter A. Victor: ECONOMICS OF POLLUTION
Grahame Walshe: INTERNATIONAL MONETARY REFORM
E. Roy Weintraub: GENERAL EQUILIBRIUM THEORY

Forthcoming

R. W. Anderson: ECONOMICS OF CRIME
G. Denton: ECONOMICS OF INDICATIVE PLANNING
J. A. Kregel: THEORY OF CAPITAL
Richard Lecomber: ECONOMIC GROWTH AND ENVIRONMENTAL QUALITY
D. Mayston: THE IDEA OF SOCIAL CHOICE
Simon Mohun: RADICAL ECONOMICS
B. Morgan: MONETARISM AND KEYNESIANISM
Christopher Nash: PUBLIC *v.* PRIVATE TRANSPORT
F. Pennance: HOUSING ECONOMICS
Nicholas Rau: TRADE CYCLES: THEORY AND EVIDENCE
M. Stabler: AGRICULTURAL ECONOMICS
E. Roy Weintraub: THE ECONOMICS OF CONFLICT AND CO-OPERATION
J. Wiseman: PRICING PROBLEMS OF THE NATIONALISED INDUSTRIES
A. Ziderman: MANPOWER TRAINING: THEORY AND POLICY

Economic Growth in Modern Britain

ANTONY PEAKER

Lecturer in Economics, University of Southampton

Macmillan

First published 1974 by
THE MACMILLAN PRESS LTD
London and Basingstoke
Associated companies in New York Dublin
Melbourne Johannesburg and Madras

SBN 333 13413 1

Printed in Great Britain by
THE ANCHOR PRESS LTD
Tiptree, Essex

Contents

Acknowledgements

The author wishes to thank David Pearce, of the University of Southampton, for encouragement and advice, and the Norwegian School of Business and Economics, Bergen, for providing facilities for the author in the summer of 1971. Special thanks go to Rita Skare Peaker, an invaluable source of encouragement and a stimulating discussant.

1 Introduction

This book is concerned with economic growth in the United Kingdom since the Second World War, and more especially with growth since the mid-1950s. The most notable fact about U.K. economic growth over these periods has been that it was considerably lower than the rates of growth of other Western European countries. During the earlier years 1947–56 this difference could be attributed to the fact that, with the aid of massive economic assistance from the United States, continental European countries were making good the immense devastation and loss of productive potential due to the Second World War. It was not until the mid-1950s that two of the major European countries, France and Germany, had managed to restore their industrial capacity to 1939 levels, and some economists have argued that it was not until the end of the 1950s that 'normalcy' was restored and valid international comparisons could be drawn; see, for example, Knapp and Lomax [29].

Throughout the 1960s, however, despite the fact that the continental European countries had clearly more than made good their wartime damage, these countries continued to maintain similar rates of economic growth to those observed in the 1950s. Growth of the U.K. economy appeared to increase, but only slightly, and the large difference in growth performance between the U.K. economy and continental European economies remained.

These facts are illustrated in Tables 1 and 2. Table 1 shows rates of growth of output per man in various Western European countries, firstly for the 1950s, and secondly for the 1960s. Table 2 shows rates of growth of gross national product (G.N.P.) for these countries in the 1960s.

Table 1

Growth of Output Per Man

Growth rate of output per man (% per annum)	*U.K.*	*France*	*W. Germany*	*Italy*	*Belgium*	*Norway*	*U.S.A.*
1950–60	1·9	4·0	5·3	4·1	2·5	3·2	2·1
1960–65	2·2	5·2	4·4	6·2	4·1	4·3	3·1
1965–70*	2·9	5·2	4·4	6·8	3·6	3·2	1·8

*(estimates)

Sources: 1950–60: Knapp and Lomax [29]; 1960–70: O.E.C.D. [39].

Table 2

Growth of G.N.P.

Growth rate (% per annum)	*U.K.*	*France*	*W. Germany*	*Italy*	*Belgium*	*Netherlands*	*Norway*	*U.S.A.*
1960–65	3·4	5·8	5·0	5·2	5·1	5·0	5·4	4·8
1965–68	2·3	4·5	3·2	6·0	3·3	4·9	4·6	4·7
1965–70*	2·4	5·4	4·4	6·3	4·2	4·7	4·4	3·7

*(estimates)

Source: O.E.C.D. [40].

The second outstanding fact about the growth of the U.K. economy in the post-Second World War period has been its cyclical nature. There has been no repetition of the extreme 'depressions' and 'booms' of the pre-1940 era, instead unemployment has constantly been low. However, fluctuations in the rate of growth have been observed and periods of full (or over-full) capacity utilisation have alternated with periods of excess capacity. Each cycle has typically been of about four years' duration. The pattern is illustrated by the figures of Table 3 which show annual growth rates of the U.K. economy year by year over this period.

This four-year cycle has been the immediate result of the policies implemented by successive British governments. It is commonly referred to as the Stop–Go cycle, and its pattern is very simple; a full description may be found in Dow [11]. Typically the 'Go' phase occurs when the balance of payments

Table 3

Growth of United Kingdom G.N.P.

Year	*G.N.P. at 1963 prices* (*Index*)	*Growth* (% *per annum*)	*Average Growth* (% *per annum*)
1956	82·3		
1957	84·0	2·06	
1958	84·4	0·48	
1959	87·6	3·80	3·0
1960	91·8	4·34	
1961	94·9	3·38	
1962	96·1	1·26	
1963	100·0	4·05	3·3
1964	105·5	5·50	
1965	108·2	2·56	
1966	110·3	1·94	
1967	112·5	1·99	
1968	116·2	3·29	2·2
1969	118·7	2·15	
1970	121·3	2·19	
1971	123·0	1·40	

Source: *National Income and Expenditure*, H.M.S.O. (1971).

is showing a surplus and the pound is strong. In such a situation there is usually excess capacity and untypically high unemployment in the British economy. In these circumstances the government chooses to 'boost' the economy. This it usually does by a mixture of policy changes. Fiscal policy is used in the, by now normal, Keynesian manner: taxes are reduced and public expenditures increased. Monetary policy is used too: credit is made more available through a reduction in the Bank Rate, through a relaxation of credit controls on the banks and through the easing of hire-purchase regulations. These measures stimulate the economy, excess capacity is absorbed and unemployment falls. The rate of growth is thus able to exceed the growth rate of capacity. In this phase the rate of growth is quite high, even relative to the other European countries.

However, this phase of high growth has, without exception since 1950, also seen a steadily worsening balance of payments. The balance-of-payments position has, in turn, led to a weaken-
ing of the £ on the for exchanges. This weakening tends to make the £ liable to suffer speculative flights of cptl out of sterling

ing of the pound on the foreign exchanges. This weakening tends to make the pound liable to suffer speculative flights of capital out of sterling. Eventually it has always become necessary for the government of the day to take some steps to improve the balance of payments.

These steps constitute the 'Stop' phase of the Stop–Go cycle. With the exception of the 1967 devaluation of the pound and the 1972 'float' all governments since the early 1950s have chosen to vary the pressure of demand on the domestic economy to control the balance-of-payments position. Reduction of this pressure reduces the rate of growth of G.N.P. and because the growth of income is curtailed the rate of growth of imports falls. The effect is to improve the balance of payments and thus to strengthen the pound on the foreign exchanges.

This gain, however, is obtained at the cost of mounting unemployment and the appearance of excess capacity. Those who invested during the 'Go' phase are now liable to find their new investments under-utilised. They are unable profitably to switch their output from domestic to foreign markets, because the reduction of home demand in no way improves their price competitiveness abroad. Some diversion from domestic to foreign markets occurs none the less as producers make more effort to sell abroad and also because, with less pressure on capacity, they will be able to quote better delivery dates. The evidence however suggests that this effect is slight.

After some time the economy reverts to the initial situation again. Each time, one must note, at a higher level of G.N.P. than at the previous such situation. The cycle now recommences. The economy is pushed into a new 'Go' phase by new government policies.

Some U.K. commentators have chosen to stress the potential role of Stop–Go in discouraging growth. When viewed in an international context this cycle appears in absolute terms to be a particularly mild one. Wilson [60] examined the variations in annual rates of growth of a number of Western economies. His results are summarised in Table 4.

It is clear that the absolute deviations about the mean growth rates in major continental European countries are comparable to those in Britain. However, it is very likely that it is not the

Table 4

Growth and Stability, 1950–64

Gross domestic product	*U.K.*	*U.S.A.*	*France*	*W. Germany*	*Italy*
Average annual rate of growth (%)	2·8	3·1	4·5	6·7	6·0
Range (i.e. difference between maximum and minimum annual rates)	5·4	2·9	4·7	2·4	5·1
Coefficient of variation	0·6	0·9	0·3	0·4	0·3

Source: T. Wilson [60].

absolute deviations which are relevant but the size of these deviations from the mean relative to the value of the mean growth rate itself. Thus an average deviation of 2 per cent per annum might be of less importance to a country growing at 6 per cent per annum than an average deviation of 1·5 per cent per annum to a country growing at 2 per cent per annum. Table 4 includes details of the relative magnitude of these ratios for the various countries: the 'coefficient of variation' as it is called. It is clear that Britain has, by this measure, suffered more heavily from the Stop–Go cycle than other countries have from *their* own cycles. This is true whether one looks at fluctuations of G.N.P., G.D.P. or of industrial production.

If one does believe that Stop–Go has had an adverse effect on the rate of growth of the British economy one must then consider whether Stop–Go was the result of political and economic mismanagement or whether it was inevitable given the low growth rate. The continually recurring balance-of-payments difficulties of the United Kingdom suggest that Britain has a chronic tendency to import more than she can export. If this is accepted, it is apparent that any government committed to maintaining the parity of the pound with other currencies will be forced to use deflation to counter the resulting adverse balance of payments.

The major reason why the United Kingdom repeatedly found herself in balance-of-payments difficulties is because the rate of price inflation in Britain has consistently outstripped that of other Western countries. The effect has been for Britain's international price competitiveness continually to deteriorate in periods when the parity of the pound was fixed, that is to say from the mid-1950s to mid-1972, with the exception of the 1967 devaluation. In 1972 the pound was 'floated' on the foreign exchanges and allowed to devalue further, and currently (in 1973) the pound is still 'floating'.

Certainly for the bulk of the period since the mid-1950s (during which the pound sterling has had a fixed international parity) it appears that money wage settlements in the United Kingdom were no higher than (and often below) similar settlements in other European countries. This is illustrated by the figures of Table 5. The higher rate of inflation in Great Britain has been related to a faster rate of growth of labour costs per unit of output, not to a faster growth of the cost of labour *per se*. The relatively high rate of increase of labour costs per unit of output occurred because of the relatively slow rate of growth of productivity, that is to say output per man.

Table 5

Growth of Hourly Rates in Manufacturing, 1959–68

	Austria	*Belgium*	*France*	*W. Germany*	*Italy*	*Netherlands*	*U.K.*
Increase %	74	79	94	86	n.a.	119	56

Source: O.E.C.D. [38].

One sees that, whatever the effect of Stop–Go on the rate of growth, it is clear that the low rate of growth has been in large part responsible for the necessity for U.K. governments to instigate and maintain the Stop–Go pattern of growth. An understanding of the reasons why growth of G.N.P. and output per man in Britain have been low is an essential prerequisite to understanding why Stop–Go has been so persistent in the United Kingdom since the mid-1950s.

The aim of this book is to examine critically the arguments

and hypotheses which economists have propounded in their attempts to explain Britain's low rate of economic growth since the mid-1950s. In historical terms U.K. growth has not been low; it appears to have been much higher since the mid-1950s than it was in the 80 years before 1940. Britain's economic growth has been low only when looked at in relation to that of the neighbouring European states. They have succeeded in accelerating their rates of economic expansion in the post-Second World War period, relative to pre-1940, very much more than Great Britain. The arguments examined in this book are therefore all comparative ones, and the central question to which the work discussed in this book has addressed itself is 'why is U.K. growth so much slower than that of other Western European countries?' rather than 'why is the U.K. growth rate *x* per cent?'

This book is non-normative. Questions about the most desirable rate of economic growth are neither posed, nor the answers, hypotheses, and discussions of economists (and others) on this matter examined. The rate of increase of an economy's product is thought worthy of study in its own right. It is also certain that discussion about what the rate of growth has been and why, is more the province of the economist *per se* than discussion of what it ought to be.

Gross national product, or output per head, or output per employee are not really satisfactory measures of 'welfare' or 'well-being'. They are crudely materialistic measures, ignoring many important factors (such as pollution and environmental damage) and omitting to include measures of the true cost of resource depletion. Intangibles such as 'the quality of life' are omitted, and so too even are measures of more tangible factors such as the quantity and quality of leisure. The attempts of economists to give even limited welfare connotations to G.N.P. (see, for example Samuelson [47] and, for a discussion of the problems, Little [33]) are based on a crude utilitarian calculus now discredited in philosophical circles. Furthermore, being aggregate measures, they can never show the distribution of material income or wealth amongst people, a factor which is clearly of paramount importance to an assessment of 'welfare' – particularly in a narrow materialistic sense.

None the less, considerable importance is accredited to measures of gross national product, output per head, and so on by politicians, commentators, and people at large. They are economic phenomena, and the study of their growth is an interesting pursuit. For these reasons it seemed both worthwhile, and in order, to prepare this book, confined as it is to an examination of why growth rates differ; and making no attempt to discuss or define optimal rates of growth.

2 A Study of Western Economic Growth

The most thorough quantitative study of Western economic growth performance is that of Denison [9]: see also [10] which is based on the earlier study and contains the salient facts. A consideration of this study is a most appropriate beginning to any attempt to assess Britain's growth performance in the context of the post-war Western world.

Denison's approach was a very basic one. He listed all the factors which could contribute to the growth of G.N.P. and then sought to assess the magnitude of each in various countries. The list of factors he used had to be confined to manageable proportions, and this involved considerable aggregation. The factors which he chose to use are, however, very reasonable.

Inasmuch as we can accept Denison's results; and this is something considered below; we can see how much growth in each country is due to increased inputs of one kind and another, how much to increased input quality, and so on. These are clearly basic factors in any appreciation of growth performance; differences between these figures for the countries studied must be explained and assessed if we are to understand why Britain's growth has been slower than that of other Western countries.

Denison's study is regrettably somewhat dated by now. He looked at growth between 1950 and 1955, and between 1955 and 1962. In the earlier period, as mentioned previously, the economies of the Western European nations were still greatly affected by the Second World War and therefore only the results pertaining to the later period are considered here. This period only extends to 1962 however. The results are therefore no more than indicative of economic conditions and performance in the West since then. Consideration of Denison's detailed examination of growth 1955–62 is still a valuable exercise for it provides concrete and detailed facts about growth in modern Europe.

Denison estimated the sources of growth of total real national income and national income per person employed, and hence the reasons behind differences in growth rates. The most basic division amongst the sources of growth is between changes in total factor input and increases in output per unit of input. These two components are, in Denison's schema, independent, and their sum equals total national income growth.*

Denison's tables are rather large and somewhat indigestible and it is useful to analyse them. Table 6 details the contributions of the three most basic factors to differential growth performance. Note the dominance, for all the European countries, of the adjusted productivity increase. This factor is the largest of the three for all these countries except Belgium, where 'irregular factors' are very slightly greater in total. The only country where it was small was the United States where productivity gain (relative to the United Kingdom) was actually the smallest of our three factors. Interestingly enough the United States was the only one of the countries studied with a growth rate per capita lower than Britain's over the relevant period. The first item in Table 6, factor inputs, is only very significant relative to the other items for one European country, West Germany.

This dominance and the strong correlation between the rate of adjusted productivity increase and the relative growth performance of the economies considered invokes interest in the components of this productivity increase. Table 7 details these components, as estimated by Denison.

Looking first at the reallocation of resources as a source of growth the predominance of the first component, the contrac-

* We shall see later how these two need not be independent, and indeed how they are commonly regarded to be interdependent. Denison himself is somewhat self-contradictory in this matter; by including (very realistically) an item for the increased realisation of economies of scale over time he is admitting that increased factor inputs, and hence output levels, do affect factor productivity.

Table 6

Differences in Growth Rates of Total National Income, by Source of Growth, 1955–62 (% per annum)

Source of growth	*Excess over U.K.*							
	U.S.A.	*Belgium*	*Denmark*	*France*	*W. Germany*	*Netherlands*	*Norway*	*Italy*
Factor inputs	0·55	−0·09	0·52	0·13	1·36	0·47	−0·46	0·33
Output per unit of input (adjusted for irregular factors)	−0·10	0·48	1·21	2·13	1·47	0·81	1·06	2·89
Total irregular factors	−0·05	0·52	0·92	0·50	0·29	0·28	0·40	0·22
Total national income	0·40	0·91	2·65	2·76	3·12	1·56	1·00	3·44

Source: Denison [9].

Table 7

Differences in Growth Rate of Output per Unit of Input (adjusted, by Source of Growth, 1955–62) (% per annum)

	Excess over U.K.							
Source of growth	*U.S.A.*	*Belgium*	*Denmark*	*France*	*W. Germany*	*Netherlands*	*Norway*	*Italy*
Contraction of agriculture	0·19	0·13	0·44	0·64	0·54	0·18	0·36	1·13
Contraction of non-farm self-employment	−0·03	0·09	0·15	0·18	0·03	0·23	0·19	0·22
Reduction of international trade barriers	−0·02	0·14	0·07	0·05	0·08	0·14	0·13	0·14
Improved allocation of resources total	0·14	0·36	0·66	0·87	0·65	0·55	0·68	1·49
Economies of scale associated with								
(a) national markets	0·03	0·11	0·26	0·24	0·25	0·16	0·14	0·30
(b) income elasticities	−0·15	0·09	0·39	0·31	0·55	0·20	0·12	0·65
(c) local markets	−0·01	0·02	0·02	0·02	0·02	0·02	0·02	0 02
Economies of scale, total	−0 13	0·22	0·67	0·57	0·82	0·38	0·28	0·97
Change in lag in application of knowledge, also errors and omissions	−0·11	−0·10	−0·12	0·69	0·00	−0·12	0·11	0·43
Grand total	−0·10	0·48	1·21	2·13	1·47	0·81	1·06	2·89

Source: Denison [9].

tion of agriculture, is clear. In all economies except two it is by far the most important of these 'reallocation factors', in the other two countries (Belgium and the Netherlands) it is of comparable magnitude to the largest factor even though not itself the largest.

The second noticeable fact is the close relationship between the two major sub-components of productivity growth. The improved 'allocation of resources' total contribution is fairly closely correlated with the 'economies of scale' total contribution. For all countries except France and the United States (in different ways) these two sub-totals sum to almost the grand total; the third component, being the change in the lag in applying knowledge, is greatly overshadowed by the other two.

The third factor to note is that out of the total contribution of economies of scale by far the largest component is that associated with income elasticities. This is true for all but two of the Western economies (Belgium and the Netherlands again); in one of these two it is still the largest factor but only just, in the other it is the second largest, although again only just.

The facts revealed by the data of Tables 6 and 7 have led some economists to argue as follows. The major component of growth is technical progress, that is to say, increase in factor productivity. This is demonstrated in Table 6 where growth of national income was considered, it is even more true of growth of national income *per capita* when the contribution of increased labour input is lost (except in so much as the age structures of the population and the work force are changing).

The prime cause of high productivity growth in West European countries, the argument continues, is the movement of labour out of low productivity agriculture into high productivity industrial or service sector employment. The increased income thus generated further compounds itself however, for the beneficiaries have a relatively high marginal propensity to spend on goods, such as consumer durables, which are produced under conditions of increasing returns to scale. The initial productivity increase thus generates a further productivity increase as input requirements per unit of output fall with the expanded production of these goods.

A major proponent of this type of argument is Professor

Kaldor [27], and we shall consider his views at some length below (in Chapter 3). Such an argument is certainly supported in no small measure by Denison's estimated figures, though his figures do not themselves contain any necessary causal relationships.

Before passing on from Table 7 we also note that the third sub-total of growth sources, the change in the lag of applying knowledge (plus an unspecified amount of 'errors and omissions'), is important in two countries according to Denison's estimates. These are France and Italy. While the overall correlation between the reallocation of labour out of agriculture and this component is weak, France and Italy are the two countries which benefited most, in terms of economic growth, from the former as well as from the latter factor. The figures do suggest that possibly radical changes in the allocation of the labour force may assist the introduction and assimilation of new production techniques. It may be that the ability of the labour force to resist innovation is weakened by relatively large changes in its composition; when, for example, trade-union strength may be eroded.

Table 8 completes the analysis of Denison's complex tables. It shows the relative contributions of factor inputs to growth performance in the various countries, alongside overall performance. Note that the direct effects of increased factor inputs are, in all cases except the United States, small in comparison to the growth of factor productivity. This is even more so if we neglect the first line of Table 8 (labour input effect) and consider the effects *per capita* of work force. These figures suggest that it will be difficult to maintain that investment rates are important determinants of growth performance unless it is possible to argue that investment rates affect productivity growth significantly.

Some economists have done so, both in theoretical and empirical frameworks, and we examine their arguments and their applicability to modern British performance in Chapter 4 below.

Recalling the similarity of U.S. economic growth to U.K. growth in the period Denison studied (1955–62), and their marked contrast in later years (1962–70), it is finally interesting

Table 8

Differences in Growth Rate of National Income, by Source of Growth, 1955–62 (% per annum)

Source of growth	*Excess (% p.a.) over U.K.*							
	U.S.A.	*Belgium*	*Denmark*	*France*	*W. Germany*	*Netherlands*	*Norway*	*Italy*
Labour input	0·62	0·31	0·33	0·09	0·59	0·33	−0·38	0·33
Capital input	−0·07	−0·40	0·19	0·04	0·77	0·14	−0·08	0·00
All other sources	−0·15	1·00	2·13	2·65	1·76	1·09	1·46	3·11
Total	0·40	0·91	2·65	2·76	3·12	1·56	1·00	3·44

Source: Denison [9].

to compare the performance of the two economies, as revealed in Tables 6, 7 and 8. Note the marked similarity in all Denison's estimates for these two economies with the exception of growth in the labour force. In *per capita* growth terms there is little to choose between the two in the period 1955–62. If nothing else then, one sees that an economy which, superficially at least, resembled the United Kingdom in its pattern of economic change can radically increase its rate of growth.

DENISON'S ESTIMATION TECHNIQUES

Having dwelt at some length on Denison's results it is only meet to examine the methods by which they were derived, for without doing so it is difficult to know how much confidence to place upon them. These methods are fully described in his longer work [9] and are quite adequately described in his shorter contribution [10]. There is an interesting discussion of them (and of Denison's empirical results) in Maddison [34].

Denison writes,

> The classification of growth sources adopted distinguishes broadly between increases due to changes in the labour, capital, and land used in production (total 'input') and increases due to changes in output per unit of input. The classification is such that, if total input in a country increases 1% a year, for example, 1% of the growth rate is shown as the contribution of inputs and the remainder as the contribution of output per unit of input. ([10] p. 238.)

Denison is clearly assuming an aggregate production function which exhibits constant returns to scale.

This procedure clashes however (as Denison recognises) with the fact of increasing returns to scale in the production of certain goods. Denison is not only aware of the phenomenon of increasing returns to scale, but, as noted above, explicitly estimates their importance as a source of differential growth performance.

In order to utilise this production function to estimate the contribution to growth of increased factor inputs in the various countries Denison needed to do two things. Firstly, he needed some way of aggregating land, labour and capital into three distinct aggregate concepts. Secondly, he needed some procedure for estimating the marginal product of each factor separately (e.g. the effect on output of a 1 per cent increase in the total employed labour force; capital stock and land utilisation remaining constant).

Both these obstacles are surmounted by employing a familiar neo-classical economic assumption, that factors are rewarded by their respective marginal products. Hence, for example, if female labour is paid 50 per cent of male labour we are enabled to aggregate the two types of labour by considering one woman worker as equal to half a male worker, and so for the aggregation of other factor inputs. Similarly we can assess the marginal product of, say, aggregate capital by looking at the payment made for the services of one unit of capital. In the aggregate, given the earlier (paradoxical) assumption of constant returns to scale in production which is necessary for the maintenance of perfect competition, this can be shown to imply that the share of total national income accruing to a factor is a measure of its marginal productivity, see, for example Solow [52]. This enabled Denison to make his calculations.

Now, not only is there some confusion as to just what Denison's production function is,* but also it is clear that his assumption of marginal productivity factor rewards – with its implicit perfectly competitive, perfectly foreseeing economy –

* Solow used a production function of the type

$$Y = A(t).F(K,L)$$

where $A(t)$ is a function of time t and accords with technical progress, $F(K,L)$ is a constant returns to scale production function in aggregate capital and aggregate labour. $A(t)$ increase with time, shifting the overall production possibility boundary upwards and outwards.

Denison's implicit formulation is similar, but confused by the fact that he wants to include increasing returns to scale. Although he estimates this latter factor to be an important growth source (as noted above), he simultaneously argues it is so unimportant as not to affect his use of a Solow-type production function [10], p. 238).

For a full account of production functions see Heathfield [20].

strains one's credulity. It is unfortunate but true that all estimates utilising aggregate production functions also use this strong assumption, its use is not peculiar to Denison. This does mean however that there is some very real doubt as to the actual relation between Denison's estimated contributions to growth and the true magnitudes. Whilst it is possible to have such doubts however, no one has successfully quantified them.

Further, more detailed examination of the procedures followed by Denison in completing his tables shows that in many cases the quality of his basic data was such that he frequently had to exercise pragmatic judgement to obtain his estimates of various factors. Indeed almost every factor presented in Table 6 in this chapter, an important summary table taken straight from Denison's work, is underlain by a series of such pragmatic judgements. Even very important growth sources, such as the reallocation of labour out of agriculture and the gains from realising economies of scale, are estimated by crude methods. Rather than terminate, they stimulate the debate.

There is one further (and very significant) reason why Denison's estimates do not successfully elucidate the process of growth in the West. This stems from the very open-mindedness of his approach. His investigation and his figures do little to lay bare the *mechanisms* of growth, to isolate and recognise the prime driving forces. It is never clear what it is that stimulates what; does a reallocation of labour out of agriculture stimulate growth, for example; or is it the desires of management and workers which demand growth and hence stimulate the movement of labour out of agriculture? What factors determine rates of technical advance? What role does investment play in economic growth? These more specific questions are not elucidated by Denison's work and other, more specific, theories must be examined to throw light on them. Denison's work does not enable us to answer satisfactorily the question as to why Britain grew less fast than her European neighbours in the later 1950s and less fast than all the other rich Western nations in the 1960s because it does not fully reveal the mechanisms of growth.

A comparison of various factors by, for example, rank correlation methods would have yielded something very similar, in terms of contributing to our understanding of growth, to Denison's more elaborate calculations. The study does however set the stage for a further examination of specific hypotheses about the mechanisms of economic growth in the West.

countries racing to achieve

3 The Contraction of Agricultural Employment

In Chapter 2 the very large contribution which the reallocation of labour from low to high productivity sectors made to explaining observed differences in growth rates was noted. High growth rates in Western European countries have been permitted (at least in part) by very considerable shrinkages in their agricultural labour forces, when measured as a percentage of total employment levels. All other studies have yielded results similar to Denison's in this respect.

Reasons why the shrinkage of the agricultural labour force in Western economies can have a powerful indirect effect on the growth of labour productivity, over and above the direct effect stemming from the reallocation of labour from low to high productivity employment, were also touched upon. It is particularly important to consider these factors closely. Some economists hold that a rapid redeployment of labour away from agricultural employment is necessary for high growth, one of the most notable being Kaldor [27]. As noted in Table 9 the proportion of the U.K. labour force in agriculture is very low, so low in fact as to preclude it from shrinking at similar rates to those observed in other Western countries. If Kaldor's hypothesis is accepted there can therefore be no hope of increasing the U.K. rate of economic growth to European levels; unless perhaps, through understanding the way in which a fast shrinking agricultural labour force causes (or permits) rapid economic growth, the United Kingdom is able to simulate the necessary effects in some other way.

Kaldor argues that high growth of manufacturing output is necessary and sufficient for high overall growth because it

Table 9

	U.K.	*Belgium*	*Netherlands*	*Norway*	*W.Germany*	*Denmark*	*France*	*Italy*	*U.S.A.*
% of total labour force in agriculture in 1950	5·4	11	14	24	25	28	29	43	12
Decline of agricultural labour force as % of total labour force (1950–62)	1·5	4·2	4·8	7·4	11·6	8·4	9·3	14·0	4·7

Source: Denison [10].

permits the realisation of economies of scale. These are widely accepted to exist in manufacturing production. He argues further that goods which are produced according to increasing returns to scale may be in income-elastic demand over the relevant range: the higher average growth of employment in high productivity sectors thereby leads, via the resultant shift in the composition of output, to further productivity gains.

Western European countries have had high rates of economic growth (Kaldor argues) because they have had an exceptionally fast rate of growth in the manufacturing sector. This latter has only been possible because these countries each had large pools of under-employed low productivity labour in agriculture. Employment in manufacturing has expanded rapidly, and the percentage of total employment in their large agricultural sectors has fallen.

The argument is not that a large agricultural labour force causes high growth, only that it permits it. There are many examples readily available to counter any suggestion that it actually causes high growth. Within Europe; Ireland, Greece, Spain and Turkey have some of the highest proportions of their labour forces in agricultural and also some of the lowest growth rates. In the period 1800–70, when the percentage of the U.K. labour force in agriculture was comparable to that of Western Europe in the 1950s and 1960s,* U.K. growth (based on the limited statistics available) appears to have been no higher than it has been in the twentieth century. Deane and Cole [8] quote growth rates of 2·9 per cent per annum for the period 1801–51 and 2·3 per cent to 2·2 per cent per annum for 1820–70. Fores [14] quotes similar figures. These rates of growth are far below those attained by modern continental European countries, indicating that a large agricultural labour force is no guarantee of fast growth.

Just as it is clear that a large agricultural labour force cannot stimulate rapid growth, so it is indisputable that it does permit

* In 1801 35·9% of the British labour force was engaged in agriculture, forestry and fishing, in 1871 the figure was 18·7%: Deane and Cole [8], p. 142.

(by its decline) the rapid growth of employment in other sectors, with consequent productivity gain and the realisation of any economies of scale this may yield. Kaldor however makes a stronger statement than this. He contends that the direct and indirect effects, stemming from the growth of manufacturing employment, account entirely for differences in growth rates. This contention is not supported by the empirical evidence.

Economies of scale can be employed to 'explain' differences in rates of economic growth in European countries but they seem unlikely to account for observed differences in real income levels. The scale of production in Great Britain and other Western countries is discussed more fully in Chapter 7, both at the industry and at the 'plant' level. Suffice it to say here that the scale and concentration of production in Britain have been high relative to other European countries, yet she no longer has the higher real incomes that economies of scale would lead one to expect. Economies of scale, an essentially static concept, can be confusing when applied in a dynamic context. Kaldor, for example, relates productivity growth in car manufacturing in Germany and the United Kingdom to *changes* in output levels – not productivity levels to output levels [27], p. 13. It seems that the quite phenomenal growth in Western Europe in the 1950s and 1960s is a dynamic pattern which is inexplicable in terms of simple static concepts.

Simple regression analysis of Kaldor's own data can be used to demonstrate that there has been no correlation, over different countries, between the growth of employment in manufacturing and growth of manufacturing productivity – counter to his own argument.* Figure 1 shows the scatter of points produced by Kaldor's data.

The same regression analysis was repeated using O.E.C.D.

* Using Kaldor's data R^2 was 0·05, and the estimated coefficient on employment growth was insignificant (t-statistic = 0·7) and small. There was no auto-correlation. The data was drawn from eleven countries for the period 1954–64. Kaldor includes two regressions in [27] (p. 12), which attempt to substantiate his argument. They are however spurious correlations because the variables he chose to use are highly co-linear.

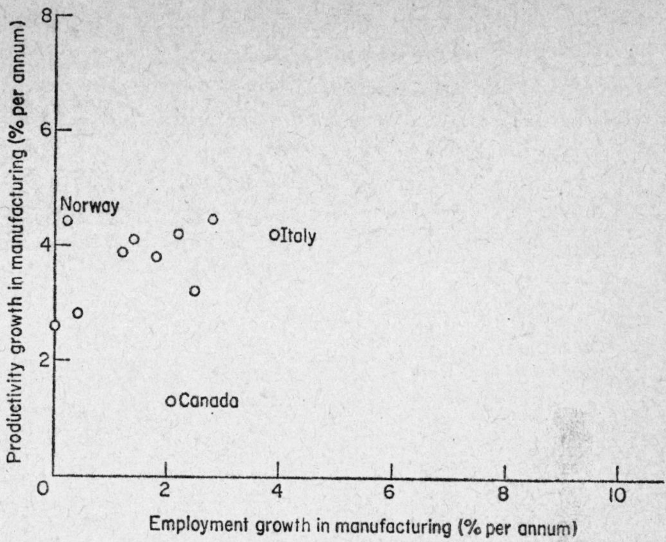

FIG. 1. Productivity and employment growth in manufacturing 1953–64

data for a different time-period. The lack of correlation was observed again.*

Denison [9] and Beckerman *et al.* [5] provide further evidence that there is no simple link between differences in growth rates and the redeployment of labour from low to high productivity sectors. The links between changes in employment patterns and rates of output growth in Western Europe seem to be part of a complex and dynamic phenomenon which simple, static theories will not unravel.

Despite the evidence noted above, which fails to support particular theses about the way in which large reallocations of labour away from agriculture might affect productivity growth rates, the fact remains that there is a strong correlation between the two factors. It is invalid to correlate total productivity growth directly against a measure of the shift of labour away from agriculture into manufacturing and services because the

* Data from O.E.C.D. [39]. R^2 was 0·07; the *t*-statistic on the employment growth parameter a mere 0·75.

direct effect on productivity of this shift is such a large part of the total gain that any correlation observed would be spurious. It is necessary to examine the relationship between the productivity growth, over and above this direct effect, and the change in the deployment of the labour force.

This relationship was examined by regression of data from various Western countries. The impact of the changed deployment of manpower was measured by the direct productivity gain attributed to this cause by Denison. The correlation was

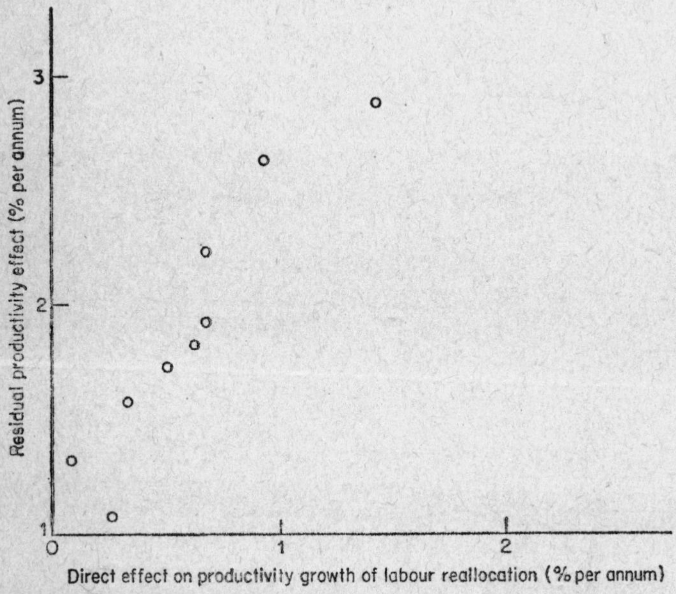

FIG. 2. Productivity growth and labour reallocation 1955–62

found to be very strong ($R^2 = 0{\cdot}87$), and the estimated coefficients were highly significant.* Figure 2 illustrates the scatter points.

* The results for the period 1955–62 were:

$$\left(\begin{array}{l}\text{Growth of labour productivity}\\ \text{less direct reallocation of labour}\\ \text{effect.}\end{array}\right) = \underset{(7{\cdot}6)}{1{\cdot}08} + \underset{(6{\cdot}8)}{1{\cdot}36}.\left(\begin{array}{l}\text{Direct re-}\\ \text{allocation}\\ \text{effect.}\end{array}\right)$$

$R^2 = 0{\cdot}87$. (Figures in parentheses are t-statistics.)

The durability of this strong correlation over time is however in some doubt. A repeat of the above regression using data for the longer period 1955–68 from the O.E.C.D. study referred to above [39] yielded $R^2 = 0{\cdot}35$, and the estimated coefficient on the 'direct reallocation effect' was insignificant.

Furthermore the correlation does not, of course, indicate any direction of causality. It seems more likely that higher growth would cause a faster shrinkage of the agricultural labour force, than vice versa. Evidence cited above showed that a large agricultural labour force does not necessarily lead to faster growth. Since Keynes, economists have become accustomed to think of investment as the prime stimulant of an economy. Investment, being primarily based on expectations and therefore to some degree independent of current economic parameters, serves to determine the growth of aggregate demand, and also of productive potential. It can therefore cause growth. Large observed declines in agricultural labour forces may be merely passive symptoms of high growth rates. A large agricultural labour force is not a necessary precondition for high growth, it is only necessary that low productivity sectors in a developed economy should not find (or construct) social and institutional barriers to their decline and replacement by new higher productivity employment.

4 Investment as a Generator of Growth

Assessments of the importance of investment as a generator of growth have almost exclusively been based on a neo-classical economic framework. Growth theory is not reviewed in this book but there are many good surveys readily available; for example Hamberg [19], Kregel [30], Solow [53]. Neo-classical growth theories suggest the following:

(i) That in the long run an economy's rate of growth will be independent of the proportion of its total output which is invested.
(ii) That the long-run growth rate is determined by the sum of the growth rate of the labour force and the rate of technical progress; and the growth of real income per head is equal to the rate of technical progress.
(iii) That over a transition period changes in the ratio of investment : total output will cause changes in the same direction of labour productivity.

Neo-classical growth theory strictly only holds for an economy with full employment, or a constant rate of unemployment. Unemployment rates in Western economies fluctuate as they pass through the trade cycle, or as government policies vary, hence neo-classical theory does not hold from year to year. (Although it can be brought toward reality in this respect by the addition of complicating factors.) In trying to test empirically the above hypotheses, therefore, one must consider lengthy time periods.

Table 10 shows, for various countries, the average annual share of investment in output for the period 1955–68, and notes how this share has varied over that time. Figure 3 plots the paths of these shares for some countries.

Table 10

Country	*Investment: total G.N.P. (average annual, measured at current prices)* (%)	*Description of path 1955–68*
Austria	23·8	An upward trend
Belgium	19·7	An upward trend
Denmark	19·5	An upward trend
France	21·6	A strong upward trend
W. Germany	24·2	Some appearance of an upward trend
Italy	20·9	An upward trend 1955–63 then a very sharp decline
Netherlands	24·3	An upward trend, strongly so 1958–68
Norway	29·4	A roughly constant trend
U.K.	16·4	An upward trend
Canada	23·8	A constant trend
U.S.A.	17·0	Very slight downward trend

Source: O.E.C.D. [41].

The general trend has been for the investment ratio to increase. The share of investment in output has however varied considerably about trend in all economies; exceedingly so in some, for example Canada, Germany, Italy.

Attempts to investigate whether or not growth rates vary with the value of the investment:output ratio have, almost without exception, been forced to compare growth rates and shares of investment over different countries, that is to conduct a cross-sectional analysis. The reason for this is paucity of data. The long-run nature of the neo-classical model, which does not pretend to explain how the investment share and the growth of output will relate from year to year in an economy, virtually precludes comparison of a single economy from one period to another. This is because one needs to compare one long period with another period. Time series analyses which have been conducted bear out the result of the cross-sectional analyses; see, for example Kuznets [31]. The studies indicate that there is no definite link between the share of investment and the rate of

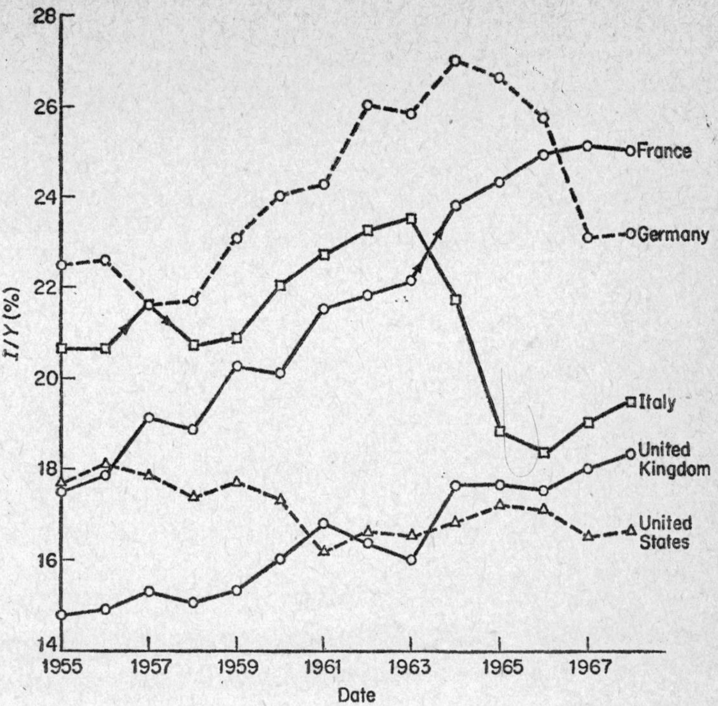

FIG. 3

growth of output. The result holds however one defines investment (e.g. gross, net, excluding construction, excluding residential), or output (G.N.P., G.D.P., output per head).

A notable recent attempt to find a relationship between investment shares and output growth rates was that of O.E.C.D. [39], in which see Appendix VI. The method of analysis was cross-sectional. Investment share and output (or productivity) growth for O.E.C.D. member countries were compared by means of linear regressions. Numerous different measures of output (and productivity) were used with numerous different measures of the investment share (e.g. excluding and including investment in dwellings).

The output growth and investment share regression was of the simple linear form:

$$\frac{\dot{Q}}{Q} = \alpha + \beta\left(\frac{I}{Q}\right)$$

where I is investment, Q is output, $\dot{Q}$ the rate of change of Q and α and β the parameters to be estimated. Table 11 summarises the results of the regressions run, using data from all countries, and Fig. 4 shows the scatter of data points.

Table 11

Regression	β	t-*statistic*	α	t-*statistic*	S.E.	R^2
1. Growth of G.D.P. (constant market prices) against gross fixed investment/G.D.P. (both at constant market prices)	0·13	1·7	1·91	1·1	1·40	0·09
2. Growth of G.D.P. (constant market prices) against gross fixed investment *less* dwellings/G.D.P. (both at constant market prices)	0·16	1·9	1·97	1·3	1·36	0·13

(20 countries)

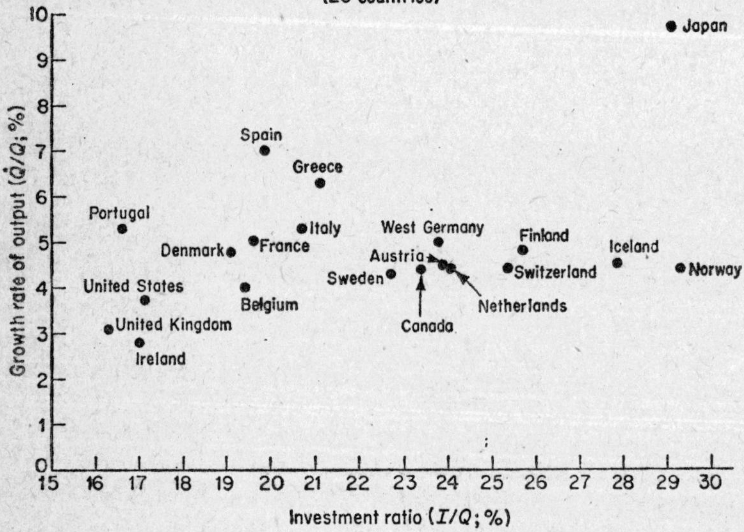

FIG. 4. Investment ratios and growth of output

It is apparent from the scatter diagram that there is no clear and well-defined relationship between rates of growth and investment shares for different countries. This is borne out by the statistical analysis. The correlation coefficients (R^2) were very small. However, the statistical analysis did indicate a positive, if weak, relationship between rate of growth and investment share. The estimated coefficient β was positive, and the *t*-statistics for the parameter (e.g. 1·7 and 1·9 above) implied that β was almost significantly different from zero (at the 5 per cent level). Although the investment share cannot be thought the only determinant of the rate of growth, these results do indicate that it may play some role. Higher investment shares are very weakly correlated with higher rates of growth and one cannot dismiss the possibility of a positive link between growth rate and investment share.

In comparing growth of output to investment share (both measured in various ways) O.E.C.D. was following a procedure used in all other investigations of the interdependence between rate of growth and the ratio of investment to output. This specification is however at variance with the neo-classical theoretical framework. This suggests that the growth rate of labour *productivity* should be independent of the investment share. The neo-classical model also suggests, as noted at the beginning of this chapter, that increases in the ratio of investment to output (the investment ratio) will, over a transition period, lead to higher rates of growth. Any influence in this respect is ignored in the simple formulation used by O.E.C.D.

Furthermore the neo-classical model used to formulate the hypotheses noted at the beginning of the chapter is an aggregative one, incorporating assumptions about the mobility of factors and the degree of competition in factor markets which preclude differences in factor productivity in different industries. It also, *a fortiori,* does not recognise the possibility of effects on productivity arising from the reallocation of labour from low to high productivity sectors. Yet we are aware that a large part of Western growth since 1945 has occurred because of just such a shift (Chapters 2 and 3). Any test of the effect of investment share on productivity growth using aggregative measures ought therefore to make separate allowance for this factor.

Examination of the levels of the investment ratios in the eleven countries of Table 10 through the years 1956–68 indicates that seven of them have had very definite and continual trend increases in this ratio. This, neo-classical theory suggests, should have led to these countries having, on average, a higher rate of output growth. Allowance for this possibility can be made by incorporating a further term in the regression.

A more correctly specified version of the model is

$$\frac{\dot{P}}{P} = \alpha + \beta\left(\frac{I}{Q}\right) + \gamma\frac{\Delta(I/Q)}{(I/Q)}$$

where $\dot{P}/P$ is corrected productivity growth, I/Q is the ratio of investment to national output, $\Delta(I/Q)$ indicates the trend change in I/Q, and α, β and γ are the parameters to be estimated.

Data for seven Western countries (Netherlands, W. Germany, Austria, France, Belgium, Denmark and Great Britain) which had shown a clearly identifiable trend in the investment ratio 1955–68 was taken from the O.E.C.D. study and used to estimate this equation. The growth of output was measured (in turn) as (a) growth of G.N.P., (b) growth of average productivity, (c) growth of productivity after allowance for gains due to the inter-sectoral reallocation of labour referred to above (i.e. $\dot{P}/P$ above). All three correlations had a high coefficient of correlation (R^2), varying from 0·83 to 0·97. In two of the three cases the coefficient on the trend in the investment ratio was insignificant. The coefficient on the investment ratio itself was always strongly significant.

These results are instructive, if a little paradoxical. They indicate that there is a correlation between rate of growth and investment share, but they also suggest that increases in the investment share in total output in any particular economy have no very definite effect on that economy's growth rate, there is no strong positive relationship linking such increases to the growth rate.

This apparent paradox may be resolved if we interpret the correlation between output growth rate and investment share as a consistency condition, rather than a causal relationship.

A high investment share is necessary for a high rate of growth, but increasing the investment share in an economy is not sufficient in itself to generate a higher rate of sustainable growth. In the United Kingdom since 1950 increased rates of investment have invariably caused the growth of aggregate demand to outstrip the growth of productivity. One is led, therefore, to ask why the United Kingdom can only maintain such relatively low productivity growth, when other development countries manage to do so much better.

There are two lines of thought which link the growth of productivity to the rate of investment. The first is that the actual pace of technical, scientific and organisational advance may be linked to the productive activities associated with creating or using capital equipment. The second is that such advances may be incorporated in the design of new plant, machinery and buildings and that technical progress can only be realised through the introduction of such modern capital equipment into service. The first line of argument is one classed as 'learning by doing', the second is an argument about the extent to which technical progress is 'embodied'.

There is considerable evidence at all levels that people and institutions 'learn by doing'. Specific economic examples have been found in aeronautical engineering, shipbuilding, machine tools, and iron manufacture; see Kennedy and Thirlwall [28] pp. 38–9. This might suggest that higher productivity (i.e. output per head) yields greater opportunities for learning by doing and hence to faster growth: and that growth leads to more growth. It does not however directly lead one to link the pace at which knowledge advances to the rate of investment *per se*. Much more directly implicated is the willingness, or otherwise, of people to learn, or to try something new, and the encouragement or discouragement they receive from the institutions of their society. These are largely social rather than economic factors. It seems much more likely that the combination of such social factors should lead to both a high rate of technical and organisational advance and to a high rate of investment, than that the reverse should happen and high investment rates affect the social factors and hence the rate at which knowledge advances.

Is technical progress embodied? The general feeling is that it is, or at least very largely so. Technical progress is really of two kinds: technical-technical progress and organisational-technical progress. Both kinds of progress permit higher outputs to be obtained from the same quantity of inputs. Technical-technical progress is often embodied by its very nature, organisational-technical progress somewhat less so. Organisational reform may not seem to require the introduction of new capital equipment 'embodying' it; but in practice companies frequently will only consider drastic change in their organisation when introducing new machinery or moving to new premises. The resistance of labour and managerial staff to organisational change often implies that it is only in the process of introducing new capital equipment that improvements in the organisation of production can be introduced. These factors introduce a strong correlation between investment in new capital stock and organisational reform.

Jorgensen and Griliches [26] in an interesting (but difficult) paper suggest that all technical progress has been embodied. Solow [54] attempted to determine the amount of fixed investment which would have to be undertaken to generate alternative growth rates assuming technical progress to be either all embodied or all disembodied. He concluded that the embodied case gave more reasonable looking conclusions. In later work [55] Solow examined growth in the United States and in West Germany and concluded again that a model incorporating embodied technical progress (at a rate of 5 per cent per annum) seemed to fit the observed data best. Intriligator also reached similar conclusions in a study of the U.S. economy; embodied technical progress of 4 per cent per annum giving the best 'fit' of predictions to observations [25]. It must be remarked however, that these empirical studies give a very poor discrimination between embodied and disembodied theories of technical progress, and later work suggests that it is quite impossible to discriminate at all in macroeconomic studies using aggregated data, see [28].

There is, therefore, only rather weak evidence to suggest that higher rates of investment might be expected to increase the rate of growth of the economy. Higher investment might increase the rate at which economically useful knowledge is gained, and might – through speeding the introduction of modern plant, machinery and buildings – increase the rate at which that knowledge is utilised. The empirical evidence above, however, suggests that the link between higher investment and higher growth is a rather uncertain and elastic one. The extent to which raising the investment ratio increases the rate of growth will depend on social and institutional factors. These could quite plausibly be the root cause of high investment rates, high productivity growth rates and high growth of *per capita* incomes in some Western economies, and of low growth rates in others (eg. the U.K.).

5 Research and Development

It is reasonable to expect that, if other things are equal, a greater commitment to R & D will accelerate technical progress and hence productivity growth. This chapter compares the R & D efforts of Western nations to see if there is any apparent failing of the United Kingdom in this sphere which may have contributed to her low growth of productivity since the mid-1950s.

Data on R & D expenditures in O.E.C.D. countries is available for the year 1963/4 [42]. The United Kingdom is shown to be a high spender in terms of R & D expenditure *per capita* and as a share of G.N.P. The United States (a much wealthier economy in *per capita* terms) has a similar profile.

Although the shares of R & D expenditure in total G.N.P.s does indicate the relative importance attached to R & D activity in difference economies it is wrong to compare directly absolute levels of R & D expenditure computed at official currency exchange rates. This is because labour of equal skill and ability does not earn the same remuneration in the different countries. Where it is relatively cheap to hire skilled R & D workers a given expenditure will command a proportionately greater collection of talents.

In order to allow for this effect one must utilise special 'research exchange rates'. It is by no means easy to compute such exchange rates, to do so requires a great knowledge of the pattern of R & D expenditure and the relative training, skill and ability of R & D personnel in the various countries. A first attempt to calculate such exchange rates has been made, though only for five of the Western countries [15]. Table 12 shows, for these countries, the relative levels of expenditure on R & D.

Table 12

	Amount		Per capita population (£ sterling)	As % of G.N.P.
	U.S. $ (million) official exchange rate	*£ sterling (million) research exchange rate (rel. to sterling)*		
U.K.	2,160	771	14·2	2·6
France	1,299	389	8·1	1·9
W. Germany	1,436	488	8·4	1·6
Belgium	137	52	5·5	1·1
U.S.A.	21,075	4,217	22·1	3·7

Source: derived from Freeman and Young [15]: and O.E.C.D. [42].

The introduction of 'research exchange rates' has little effect on the relative expenditures of the European countries *vis-à-vis* themselves. The significant effect is the reduction of the *per capita* expenditure on R & D in the U.S.A. relative to the European countries, it is still however by far the greatest of them all. The real expenditure *per capita* of population on R & D in the various countries certainly do not relate to observed productivity growth as one might expect. The heaviest spenders on R & D (the U.K. and the U.S.A.) have had the lowest *per capita* growth rates.

A possibility is that the heavy R & D spenders devote too many resources to basic, or to applied R & D. O.E.C.D. investigated the allocation of R & D expenditure to basic research, applied research, and to development. Basic research is work undertaken primarily for the advancement of scientific knowledge, with no specific practical application in view; applied research is similar except that there is a specific practical aim in view; and development is the use of the products of basic and applied research directly to innovate and improve existing procedures. Measured in percentage terms, the emphasis on basic and applied research in the United Kingdom is very low and the emphasis on development strong. In this respect the structure of the R & D effort more closely resembles that of the United States than that of the other European countries. The major disparity between R & D balance in the advanced industrial nations is due primarily to their differing emphasis on applied research *vis-à-vis* development, the variations in the percentage of expenditure devoted to basic research are much less.

This imbalance may have a significant effect. Balance can reduce the need to import knowledge from abroad and would also, most importantly, facilitate any such transfer of knowledge. The evidence is that a great deal of scientific knowledge in Western nations is gained from abroad. In order to be capable of finding the knowledge it wants, and of using this, it seems that a country must itself have people working in the relevant fields. These people can attend conferences and symposia, read and present papers, study patents and so on. Despite modern developments in communication direct personal contact still seems to be very important in the dissemination of scientific knowledge. Table 13 illustrates this. It details the importance of various modes of communication in the dissemination of R & D work on twenty different projects in the United States. It may be that Britain's relative neglect of applied research has, despite her relatively large overall R & D effort, served to impede the flow of important information into the United Kingdom.

Table 13

Method of Knowledge Transfer of R & D Events Leading to Twenty Weapons Systems (U.S.A.) (percentages)

	Mode of Transfer		
Category	*Personal contact*	*Publication or report*	*Seminar or Symposium*
Science	45	53	2
Technology			
(a) New materials, concepts, functions	64	33	3
(b) Design technique	79	21	0
(c) Manufacturing techniques	77	23	0

Source: *Technology in Retrospect and Critical Events in Science*, National Science Foundation

A further apparent imbalance in R & D effort is found when

we consider in more detail the breakdown of R & D effort by industry. Table 14 details the R & D expenditure, as a percentage of total R & D expenditure, of three major industries in various countries. There is some evidence here to suggest that the United Kingdom is overcommitted to R & D in the aircraft/aerospace industry, and is weak in chemicals. This hypothesis is stressed by Peck [43]. However, it is not unnatural that different countries should emphasise different aspects of R & D work. This is what one would expect from international trade theory and the relative specialisation of economies.

Table 14

Percentage of Total R & D Expenditure in Various Industries, 1963/4

	Aircraft	*Electrical and electronics*	*Chemicals, including petroleum refining and drugs*
U.K.	28·4	19·8	13·2
U.S.A.	38·2	19·7	12·1
France (1964)	22·4	26·0	17·9
W. Germany	n.a.	28·2	32·0
Italy	n.a.	20·5	25·4
Belgium	1·4	17·0	40·9
Norway	n.a.	16·2	16·2
Sweden	18·6	22·5	9·4
Japan	n.a.	26·0	26·2

In measuring the manpower devoted to R & D we have taken no account of possible variations in the nature of professional manpower in industry in the various countries. One facet of this is that, in the United Kingdom, the proportion of scientists amongst total engineers and scientists in industry is abnormally high. Table 15 details the relevant proportions for a number of countries.

It is clear that the United Kingdom has an abnormally low proportion of her total professional engineering and scientific manpower in industry and also that, within industry, there is an abnormal dependence on scientists compared to engineers.

This relative dependence on scientists in Britain undoubtedly reflects supply conditions, themselves being determined by

Table 15

Percentage Distribution of Engineers and Scientists, and Proportion in Industry, 1959

	Engineers	*Scientists*	*No. of technicians per scientist or engineer*	*Percent of total scientists and engineers in industry*
U.K.	54	43	1·69	42
U.S.A.	71	25	1·40	74
Belgium	77	14	2·82	54
France	67	21	1·63	52
Netherlands	80	12	–	n.a.

Source: Peck [43], p. 451.

social forces. In Great Britain the scientist has much higher status than the engineer, and there is here a notable difference to continental European countries. In general it is the better students who choose to study science in preference to engineering, and there is in fact considerable difficulty in filling some U.K. degree courses in engineering. Training must however have some influence on character, and it may be that Britain's high use of scientific manpower in R & D work has led to it being too pure, too high quality, and insufficiently commercially orientated. Indeed the same social forces which lead to the unpopularity of engineering studies and to the low status of the engineer as a professional in the United Kingdom are likely to encourage such tendencies in R & D. Great Britain's relatively high dependence on scientists and low use of engineers may then have contributed to her poor R & D 'pay-off', though it is the social factors which are the more basic. We will return to these in Chapters 7 and 8.

It has been suggested that Britain places an undue reliance on technicians *vis-à-vis* professional engineers and scientists. The figures of Table 15 do not support this hypothesis in the European context, though it is true that all European countries use more technicians per professional than does the United States. This probably reflects the stringency attached to the attainment of a professional qualification in Europe.

The evidence related in this chapter offers some support for the hypothesis that Britain's low growth rate is due to her neglect of R & D, or to the misuse of her R & D resources. Certain factors in this sphere may contribute to the low U.K. rate of growth, but it seems most unlikely that they offer sufficient explanation.

6 Industrial Organisation

Output is produced by industry, and the growth of an economy's output is therefore going to be some function of the form and quality of it's industrial organisation. The present chapter looks at industrial organisation in the United Kingdom, and how it compares to that of other developed Western nations, it also investigates the degree to which industrial organisation might be responsible for the relatively poor growth performance of the British economy since the Second World War.

As is often the case with significant economic concepts it is very difficult to assess such a complex phenomenon as 'industrial organisation'. This chapter is concerned primarily with the degree of concentration of production in the various major industries and in the economy as a whole. This measure of organisation, whilst only one of many, is one which is commonly and widely used. It is a statistic which may be applied to all kinds of productive activity and one which may be compared internationally. It is also, and very relevantly, one which it is not too difficult to obtain. Of course its very simplicity and generality do detract from its analytical and descriptive powers. The consequences of, and reasons for, high concentration are not necessarily the same in one industry as another. As far as is possible, therefore, it is necessary to go beyond this one simple measure, and when it is not possible to do so in quantitative terms to indicate perceived tendencies. The measure of industrial concentration is useful in looking broadly at industrial organisation.

A number of studies have attempted to compare the concentration of industries in Britain and the United States, very few, however, concerned themselves with the relative positions, in this respect, of the United Kingdom and other continental European countries. Both the United States and Britain, we recall, had similar and low rates of growth in the 1950s. In the 1960s however the rate of economic growth of the United States was much higher than that of the United Kingdom and quite comparable to those of continental European countries (see Chapter 1).

There is always a certain arbitrariness in defining the amount of concentration in an industry. The most widely used measures are the percentage of total industry output produced by, and the percentage of total industry employment in, the three largest firms, but other similar measures have also been used. In practice the relative degrees of concentration, either between industries or between countries, varies with the definition used, and there is, therefore, always a certain ambiguity in judging the relative position.

This sensitivity may be illustrated by looking at a particular study. W. G. Shepherd [50] found, for 1951, that 7·5 per cent of British manufacturing industry was in industries where the three largest firms controlled more than 60 per cent of employment whereas the equivalent figure for the United States was 12·4 per cent. However, if cars, trucks and buses were considered as one industry – the motor vehicle industry – this latter figure drops to 7·3 per cent: a very significant change, both absolutely and relatively.

Allowing for such problems of measurement the only safe conclusion it seems possible to draw from the various studies is that there is little evidence for higher concentration of industrial production in Britain than the United States, though there is some indication that production might be more concentrated in the former than the latter, see, for example Sargent Florence [13], Shepherd [50] and Bain [2]. It is also probably true to say that conditions of near monopoly are more common in the United Kingdom.

These conclusions are borne out by Bain's very thorough study of eight Western countries including Britain and the United States. Bain's work is of the highest standard and is notable for using a sample of consistently defined industries. It is quite difficult to define such industries, hence the limited sample size for some countries, but one feels much safer using data based on them; experience indicates that very different types of industry are often included in the same categories by statisticians. Table 16 details Bain's findings as to concentration in major industries in the United States, Great Britain, France, Italy, Canada and Sweden. It is clear that there are no very significant differences overall between the different countries, and not only between Britain and the United States.

As a measure of monopoly power accruing to major producers, concentration of production is of course only very rough. As we indicated above it is quite sensitive to changes in definition and, further, it is only a measure of the largest firms in an economy relative to the size of the industry in that econo-

Table 16

Concentrations in Production[a] in Six Countries During the 1950s

Industry	*U.S.A. four-firm concentration ratio*	*Three-firm concentration ratio*				
		U.K.	*France*	*Italy*	*Canada*	*Sweden*
Electric lamps	93	56	–	–	–	–
Explosives	72	91	–	–	–	–
Distilled liquors	64	73	–	–	–	–
Steel ingots	64	32	41	47	–	49
Aircraft	47	47	57	–	78	–
Plastics	47	51	–	–	–	–
Shipbuilding	43	23	76	67	–	–
Flour and meal	40	46	49	–	35	33
Petroleum refining	32	93	72	40	61	100
Cement	31	90	53	46	–	80
Pulp mills	29	–	–	–	–	32
Canned and preserved fruit, vegetables	28	21	14	–	32	–
Beer and ale	27	11	25	–	–	–
Paper and paper board	19	19	14	19	–	33

[a] Percentage of industry controlled by largest three (or four) firms in the industry.

my – the facts that an industry might be under pressure from imported goods, or might itself be dependent on exporting, are totally neglected. None the less it is fairly clear that the relative degree of concentration in U.K. industry can be no explanation in itself for the United Kingdom's poor growth rate.

It is of interest too to know if the degree of concentration in production is changing, and if so in what direction and how fast. Increasing concentration may lead to faster growth in the the short run, as new economies of scale are realised, and to lower growth in the long run as new near monopolists become secure, settled and complacent; though this later development is by no means certain to occur as they may utilise their monopoly profits and comparative security to press ahead with R & D and technological progress.

The evidence is that concentration is generally increasing though not at such a rate as to contribute any very noticeable short-run effect to growth rates. The main method by which this is occurring in Europe, including Britain, is by merger: the joining of two, often very large firms. Notable examples of this are the General Electrical–A.E.I. merger in the United Kingdom, concentration in the car industry, the Agfa–Gevaert link-up and the Dunlop–Pirelli link. Descriptions of this process in Britain may be found in Armstrong and Silberston [1] and Shepherd [51]. See also Utton [59].

As noted, concentration in production does not seem to vary significantly between the Western developed nations. The measure of concentration however only gives an indication of the size of firms relative to their domestic markets, and a vaguer indication of their size relative to total markets. Equal degrees of concentration in markets of very different sizes imply that firms within those industries are of very different sizes. It is the size of firms and of their plants which indicate whether economies of scale are being fully utilised, or whether further economies of this kind might be possible if production were yet further concentrated. An industry supplying a smaller market might find its growth performance handicapped as it would be unable to realise fully the contribution of economies of scale and, possibly, of modern capital-intensive technology.

Britain is not penalised in this respect by the size of her

markets, but it is necessary to investigate if the United Kingdom is in some way failing to realise the possibilities of using large plants to supply her large markets. For evidence on this we turn again to Bain's study, [2]; see also Pratten, Dean and Silberston [46]. For each of up to thirty-four different industries in the various countries Bain measured the average number of employees in the twenty largest plants. His results are summarised in Table 17, and although pertaining to the 1950s they remain indicative.

Table 17

Average Sizes of the Twenty Largest Plants in up to Thirty-four Industries Expressed Relative to United States Value (U.S.A. = 100)

	No. of industries covered	*Median plant size (relative)*	*Range of relatives (largest–smallest)*	*% of industries with plant size relative of 70 or above*
U.S.A.	34	100	100–100	100
U.K.	32	78	24–131	53
France	31	39	11–89	19
Italy	32	29	8–70	6
Canada	14	28	5–117	14
Sweden	27	13	6–43	0

It does seem that generally plants are smaller in Britain and Europe than in the United States, but it is also apparent that plants in the United Kingdom are generally far larger than in other Western European countries. This suggests that large plants are far from sufficient by themselves to generate high growth in an economy (not too unexpectedly) and also that the United Kingdom's potential for increasing her growth rate as a result of realising further economies of scale by further concentrating production is small, and far less than that of the other European nations.

The negative, but none the less valuable, conclusion to this section is that such broad factors as concentration in industry and plant size offer no explanation of Britain's poor growth performance in the 1950s and 1960s. Judged by the size of her industrial plants Britain has already had ample opportunity to benefit from economies of scale, and further increase in plant size is likely to have a more important effect on growth rates in continental Europe than in the United Kingdom. Whether or not the United Kingdom has actually reaped the potential benefits of large-scale production is still an open question however. If she has not then the blame must be laid on bad management and organisation and/or on the quality or nature of the labour force.

7 The Quality of British Management

The assessment of such a vague concept as 'the quality of management' is fraught with difficulty. It is not possible to make definitive statements, particularly because it is necessary to consider these factors very broadly. Impressions have to be examined as well as 'hard' facts, and interpretation is bound to be a major difficulty. This path, from 'harder' to 'softer' facts is commonly followed in debating economic growth, though economists appear often to have placed less emphasis on the 'softer' facts than seems merited. Discussion of them is frequently restricted to a mere addendum to a complex analysis of hard facts; Denison, for example, [10] resorts in the last analysis to an apparent persistent over-manning and inefficiency in U.K. industry as being the cause of her relatively low growth rate and real-income levels. Other writers, such as Landes, Hobsbawm and Shanks have, on the other hand, stressed the importance of these 'softer' facts in explaining the performance of the British economy [32, 23, 49].

In order to discuss the quality of management one needs some criteria of good management. The criteria which have been used include profitability (usually as a rate of return on capital), attitudes to technical change, the use made of managerial and organisational science, behaviour toward risk taking and capability in marketing. Good management presumably implies that the managerial team succeeds in fulfilling its own aims, use of the criteria mentioned above rather begs the question as to what these aims are. A considerable debate has been conducted over the years as to the aims of modern corporate firms, and it has not been satisfactorily resolved. The criteria which commentators have used in trying to assess managerial quality, and which are mentioned above, are those which figure in some positive role in most formulations of these aims. They represent the characteristics of management which are most likely to accelerate growth and change in the economy.

Studies of relative profitability are difficult to conduct. This is firstly because real profitability is very difficult to measure, particularly in inflationary periods such as the 1950s and 1960s, and secondly because it is difficult to tell if one is comparing like with like, as different firms use different accounting practices.

The most well known study is that of Dunning comparing the profitability of U.K.-owned companies and U.S.A. subsidiary companies in the United Kingdom [12]. Dunning finds that the U.S. subsidiaries in Britain earn substantially higher after-tax profits on net assets than their U.K. competitors do, industry by industry. Table 18, taken from Dunning's paper, gives details for 1958 and 1961. It is felt that differences in accounting practice are not responsible for the recorded differences in profitabilities, and that the profitability of the U.S. subsidiaries is not swelled to such an extent by the inflow of free R & D from the parent companies as to annul these very substantial differences; see Caves contribution to [6]; though not everyone is convinced of this [7].

Dunning further found, from a sample of seventeen subsidiaries and seventeen competing domestically owned firms that profitability is the greater the more 'Americanised' the company is; wholly owned subsidiaries did better than joint ones and those with American managing directors did better than those with British ones. Labour productivity and capital per head were higher in the subsidiaries than in the indigenous companies; expenditure on marketing and distribution was higher and on administration lower, as a proportion, of total sales revenue.

These results are persuasive evidence as to managerial shortcomings in Britain. Both the financial analysis and the sample survey (small though the sample was) point in the same direction. U.K. management seems, under similar conditions, to be either less capable or less interested in making money than its counterpart in (or from) the United States.

Table 18

Rates of Return on Net Assets, by Industry, U.K. Companies and Sample of U.S. Subsidiaries, 1958 and 1961

	Before-tax rates of return on net assets			
	1958		*1961*	
Industry	*United States*	*United Kingdom*	*United States*	*United Kingdom*
Chemicals, etc.	17·9	16·6	17·4	16·8
Metal manufacture	31·2	19·3	18·3	17·0
Non-electrical engineering	21·9	20·3	26·8	18·7
Electrical Engineering	43·2	19·7	21·8	18·7
Metal goods[a]	30·0	23·0	25·9	20·2
Textiles, footwear, clothing	19·1	13·5	7·8	17·3
Food, drink, tobacco	37·2	19·3	31·6	18·2
Paper, printing, etc.	21·1	17·7	17·3	17·2
Vehicles	25·7	24·6	21·0	16·7
Other manufacturing	21·4	19·6	25·2	19·1
Total manufacturing	24·0	18·8	21·1	17·8

Source: Dunning [12].

[a]'Not elsewhere specified'.

It is difficult however to relate differences in managerial quality or attitudes to relative rates of economic growth. For example, during the 1950s the American economy grew at a rate very similar to Britain's, during the 1960s it grew considerably more quickly. Studies of attitudes in management suggest that German and American managers have similar attitudes and tend to group French and Belgian managers with British ones in this respect [18], yet both France and Germany have had very rapid economic growth throughout the 1950s and 1960s.

Systematic differences have been noted in attitudes towards risk taking by management [18, 4]. Again the French and the British tend to be grouped together as being averse to risk taking, whilst German and U.S. management are portrayed as being keen to take risks (provided the possible pay-off is high). Once more this rather founders as an explanation for growth differentials on the very different growth performances of the

British and French economies. The same may be said of nepotism or over-rigid promotion rules within industry [45].

The important difference between France and Britain seems to be the attitudes of those in positions of power to technology. Technical expertise is very highly regarded in France, and the technologist has a high status in the community. The top management of private and public sectors is conducted by personnel, largely educated at the Polytechniques, with a strong pro-technological bias in their attitudes. The movement of personnel from the head of the Civil Service into prominent positions in the private sector has been considerable. In all these respects we find a notable divergence between France and Britain.

There is some feeling that Britain lags in applying management science, even relatively simple tools such as investment appraisal by discounted cash flow methods being used only by a small proportion of firms [37]. It could well be that resistance to innovation in management methods is relatively strong in the United Kingdom. Resistance to such innovation might spring from two well-recognised factors in British industry and the Civil Service. The first is the relative lack of technologists in British industry and their lack of power in the Civil Service, and the second is the wider anti-technical bias found in Britain (somewhat paradoxically as the U.K. economy is more dependent on the products of advanced technology than other Western European nations).

The Civil Service in recruiting its Administrative Class – the group within the Service who possess the prime decision making roles – has preferred to recruit the intelligent, widely educated and non-technical man. A major source of such recruits over the years has been Arts and Classics graduates of the oldest Universities: Oxford and Cambridge.

The shortcomings of this method of recruiting, and its concomitant bias against technically qualified candidates, have been recognised [16]. The nature of the Civil Service's role has changed very considerably since this recruiting procedure was initiated. Since the Second World War, the role, power and size of the Civil Service have grown immensely. The responsibilities of the Service (and of other public servants, for example in the nationalised industries) have expanded into many new, and increasingly technical, fields. Its post-1945 concern with planning and controlling the economy, its involvement with private industry, the nationalised sectors, regional economic development, town and regional planning, the welfare state, etc. is of an entirely different nature and magnitude to pre-1939. In all these spheres professional training and technical expertise are required. There is a very large technical civil service; composed of scientists, engineers, statisticians, planners, etc.; but the influence it has been able to wield over actual decisions has probably been too small. The procedure used to recruit the Administrative Class, and the accompanying anti-technological ethos it reflects and supports, may well have impeded the application of scientific method to management in the public sector.

The position in British industry differs from that in the Civil Service. There appears to be a considerable bias in recruiting against all prior, formal higher education and a marked preference for training people on the job. Only of late has the intake of university graduates as trainees tended to increase and move towards the levels found in comparable industries in other Western developed nations; and the selection methods employed have been criticised as bearing too close a resemblance to methods currently being abandoned by the Civil Service: see Woodward [61], Postan [45] and Granick [81].

The bias against prior formal technical training for management, and the ethos of British management – both public and private sector – seems rather unique amongst the rich Western nations; and it is most strange when one recalls that Britain is one of the most technologically advanced of these nations.

Some indication of the manner in which U.K. use of professional scientific and technical personnel differs from that of other Western nations may be gained from Table 15 of Chapter 5 (detailing the allocation of engineers and scientists to industry) and Table 19 below, which shows the percentage of establishments in various major industrial groupings employing technically qualified manpower.

The percentage of establishments in these major industries in the United Kingdom employing technically qualified staff is very low relative to other countries, and this is not due to

Table 19

Percentage of Establishments Employing Technically Qualified Personnel, Seven Countries, by Industry, 1955–56 Survey

	Industry		
	Metals	*Food*	*Electrical*
United Kingdom	31	37	45
United States	69	48	72
Austria	73	57	75
Belgium	68	55	n.a.
W. Germany	67	n.a.	n.a.
Italy	72	49	n.a.
Norway	63	n.a.	72

Source: Peck [43].

greater concentration in British industry. This must imply some considerable handicap in the dissemination of technical knowledge and the use of relatively crude methods of obtaining information from the market and the shop floor for the management of many companies.

Sluggishness in adapting to changed circumstances, and reticence to adopt new organisational forms, management methods and scientific approaches on the part of the British are not, it has been powerfully argued, something new. Evidence of sluggishness, of inability to adapt, of failure to utilise new organisational forms and of failure to harness science properly as a servant of industry in the British economy of the late nineteenth century is well documented. In the greater part of that century Britain was commercially and industrially the world leader, but by the turn of the century her supremacy – particularly in industry – was being powerfully challenged by Germany. New industries were springing up; chemicals and electrical engineering being the most significant. These industries were dependent on science in a way that the engineering of Victorian Britain, with its crude brashness, was not. There was little room within them for the individual inventor and empiricist who, with a dash of genius and a lot of energy, could devise new products and make major advances. Instead there was the need for a careful scientific approach, for planning and for a concerted effort, often over a lengthy time period, by a team of workers. Organisation was all-important, not only in design and invention but also in running new forms of highly capital-intensive industrial plant. Britain, it would seem, only adopted these new approaches with great reluctance and sought instead to protect its colonial markets from Germany's successful exploitation of science-based industry, and from her aggressive marketing and sales effort, through preferential trading agreements; see Landes [32] and Hobsbawm [23]. There is evidence that it was not the technical challenge of the new industries which thwarted Britain (as one might expect given the splendid history of her own technical inventiveness) but managerial reluctance to try something new, to adopt new organisational forms and to utilise more aggressive marketing and sales techniques; see Landes, Hobsbawm, McCloskey [36]. The tremendous drive and desire to try new things possessed by the earlier Victorians seem to have been lost in the complacency and self-congratulatoriness of imperial power.

Although the cost of twentieth-century wars to Britain has been vast she has always been on the victorious side in major conflicts. The British Isles have not been a major battleground (as France and Germany have) in either of the two great wars, nor did she suffer disruption and destruction to anything like the same extent as they did. Because of this it may be that Britain has still not overturned these attitudes of the late nineteenth century, whilst the countries of continental Europe have been led to question and change on account of the traumas they have suffered. This hypothesis is stressed by Fores [14] though he appears to understate the amount of change in institutions and attitudes which undoubtedly has occurred in Britain. Further interesting ideas about and comments on Britain's progress in the nineteenth century and through the twentieth century are to be found in Hobsbawm [23].

There is thus a considerable weight of evidence, borne out by many commentators, that British management, and the social structure from whence it comes, are not as conducive as they might be to the furtherance of Britain's economic growth; and that the United Kingdom may be penalised in this respect relative to other rich Western nations.

8 Trade Unions, Collective Bargaining and Labour Attitudes

Like the rest of the book this chapter is concerned with influences on the growth of output. It therefore does not consider the impact of labour attitudes, unions, and the collective bargaining framework on rates of inflation but examines how these three interdependent phenomena may have contributed to the low growth of productivity in the United Kingdom since 1950. To do so it is necessary to compare, as well as is possible, the relevant aspects of these phenomena in various Western countries.

The framework of collective bargaining in the United Kingdom is quite unique amongst Western nations. This uniqueness stems from the extent to which negotiation in the strongly unionised sectors is decentralised, most especially in blue-collar sectors. Trade unions in Britain are organised, basically, at two levels. There is an official union establishment of staff officers and elected chief officers. This official union is almost invariably affiliated to the T.U.C. There is also an unofficial (and unpaid) union system. The backbone of this system is the shop steward. He is an employee who, in each plant, is elected to represent the interests of union members to the plant management. Within a plant each union with a sizeable group of workers will have its own shop steward. In large multi-union plants these stewards usually participate in a joint committee to co-ordinate, at least to some extent, their activities. The role of the shop steward in bargaining is described in McCarthy [35].

In the United Kingdom the shop steward, negotiating at work-place level, has a remarkable degree of autonomy. A two-tier system of bargaining has developed. National negotiations, between employers' federations and national unions, set minimum standards of pay, etc. Beyond this agreement, typically very narrow in scope, individual employers bid higher rates for scarce labour, and plant-based union organisations (led by shop stewards) seek better terms from their respective employers.

National trade unions in the United Kingdom are, in themselves, weak. They lack personnel and financial resources. Involvement with the Establishment in general and with the Labour Party absorbs the time of many key national leaders. They find themselves busy on committees and commissions and have proportionately less time and energy available for the affairs of their own unions. National unions do influence their members and their stewards by their control over the dissemination of information, by their accepted leadership role, and by their rules.

There are strong grounds for believing that the two-tier system of bargaining has encouraged the perpetuation of low productivity growth in Britain. The reasons for this belief are as follows:

(i) The system enables inefficient firms to survive. Nationally negotiated rates are typically at such a level as to allow the weaker firm to survive. The second tier of negotiation then allows workers in profitable firms to try to obtain higher payment. The two-stage negotiating procedure permits flexibility of wage payments to suit the efficiency of firms.

(ii) The quality of bargaining and dispute settlement has been lowered due to lack of skilled personnel on the union side. This shortage arises for two main reasons associated with the two-tier system. Firstly, employees associate themselves only with the unions' plant-level activities, and are therefore unwilling to pay realistic dues. This has left the national unions short of the financial resources necessary to hire skilled economic and negotiating personnel in competition with the employers. Secondly, the number of shop stewards is so large that it is not possible to give them an optimal level of training and education in broader matters relevant to the negotiations in which they are continually involved.

(iii) Divorce of effective negotiation from national unions has meant that one cannot make the national unions accountable for the behaviour of their shop stewards. This has precluded the construction of an effective legal framework to cover collective agreements such as is found in all other Western countries. British industrial relations stand out because they are so little regulated by law, and the 1971 Industrial Relations Act (commented on below) is an attempt to change this.

(iv) The two-tier system has meant that national agreements tend to be narrow in scope. They (typically) only cover minimum rates of pay and minimum holiday provision and, unlike continental European practice, do not seek to delineate a framework of rules within which management is left with considerable initiative to institute change. The result has been that management has to negotiate more frequently than otherwise when it wishes to change anything connected with production in the plant. Conditions of work, and permissible managerial flexibility, are not specified by the national agreements. Some observers have suggested that this constant need for new negotiations presents a check on managerial initiative, and has been actively used to check productivity growth; see for example Ulman [58].

The relatively great importance of the plant-bargaining tier (i.e. the shop stewards) in the United Kingdom is indicated by the high incidence of unofficial strike activity. In the later 1960s, it has been estimated, 90 per cent of stoppages and 70 per cent of working time lost due to strikes were attributable to unofficial action [22]. Strikes are not the only form of labour action however; go-slows, non-co-operation, and refusal to bend the rules are also used effectively. The statistics on strike action (themselves imperfect due to the difficulties of defining and recording strikes) are therefore useful only as indicators.

They indicate that labour militancy in Britain is not particularly high. The Royal Commission on Trade Unions and Employers' Associations [22] conducted an international comparison of strike activity. They compared data on the number and duration of stoppages of work in various countries over three fairly typical years, 1964–6. In terms of the number of stoppages per 100,000 employees, the average number of persons involved in a stoppage, and the number of working days lost per 1000 employees, the United Kingdom was about average. There was some indication that the average duration of each U.K. strike was somewhat lower than average, and the frequency of strikes somewhat higher, but these discrepancies were not very great. A selection of strike statistics from the Royal Commission's report is shown in Table 20.

Table 20

Comparative International Strike Statistics, 1964–6

	No. of stoppages per 100,000 employees	*Average no. of persons involved per stoppage*	*Average duration of each stoppage in working days*	*No. of working days lost per 1000 employees*
United Kingdom	16·8	340	3·4	190
Australia	63·8	350	1·8	400
Belgium	7·0	680	9·2	200
Canada	15·8	430	14·0	970
Denmark	5·5	370	7·3	160
France	21·8	1090	0·8	200
W. Germany	n.a.	n.a.	3·6	10
Italy	32·9	720	5·3	1170
Japan	7·6	1040	2·9	240
Netherlands	2·2	370	2·4	20
New Zealand	26·8	250	2·1	150
Norway	0·6	100	26·0	5
Sweden	0·5	570	15·4	40
United States	13·2	470	14·2	870

Source: Hyman [24].

A full discussion of strikes in Great Britain, covering their nature and incidence, is included in Hyman [24]; see also Turner [56] for a critical analysis of international strike statistics.

As noted above the two-tier system of bargaining found in Britain is quite unique amongst the rich countries of the Western world. The United Kingdom is also the only one of these countries in which collective agreements have not been legally binding. Very largely this is because it is almost, if not totally, impossible to introduce such legal constraints effectively in a two-tier bargaining system of the U.K. type. The 1971 Industrial Relations Act does contain provision for making collective agreements legally binding, if both parties consent to this, and it does attempt to make unions responsible for the unofficial action of their members.

The first of these two provisions has not yet proved popular; no major negotiated agreements have been made legally binding. The second provision noted above was put to the test in the disputes over the loading and unloading of containers by non-dock labour in 1972. The industrial action, which involved members of the Transport and General Workers Union, consisted of the unofficial blacking of certain cold stores and transport firms which used non-dock labour to load and unload marine containers. Although the action was unofficial the National Industrial Relations Court held the T.G.W.U. responsible. The union was heavily fined and the blacking forbidden. Although the judgement against the union was then reversed in the Court of Appeal, the fines were subsequently reinstated by the House of Lords (26 July 1972). The union was held responsible for the unofficial action of its stewards and its members.

This judgement appears to be a very important one. Despite the fines and court orders the blacking did continue. The central union was not able to discipline and control its members. This is quite typically the case where the two-tier bargaining system exists. The fact that unions are to be held responsible for the unofficial actions of their members under the Industrial Relations Act must provide a strong incentive for them to strengthen their organisations and to exert more effective control over their members. This will require the abolition or drastic modification of the two-tier system of bargaining which implies, as shown below, a move toward a more typical European form of union organisation.

A comparison of the U.K. system with labour and labour movements in other Western countries reveals interesting differences. A useful survey is found in Balfour [3].

Union membership is high in all Western European countries except France and Italy. Unions in these countries have low membership (e.g. 20 per cent of workers in France), fluctuating membership and very low financial resources. Worker solidarity and union strength have quite possibly not developed because of the strength of tradition and the large influx into industry of peasants from the land in these countries (see Chapter 3). The unions have not been permitted to play any constructive direct role in governing the country. Collective bargaining in these countries has been almost non-existent and wage determination has been dominated by the government and the employers. Labour has exerted a direct effect by political demonstration rather than negotiation (e.g. the demonstrations and strikes in Paris, 1968).

Belgium, Denmark, W. Germany, the Netherlands and Norway all have a very high proportion of their labour forces unionised. The process of collective bargaining is highly centralised, the unions are financially strong and they are involved directly in governing the country.

The United Kingdom also has a very high proportion of its labour force unionised. The nature and behaviour of its union movement are however very different to those in the other Western countries with numerically strong trade unions. The national unions are financially very weak and consequently under-staffed. Collective bargaining is highly decentralised (uniquely so, as noted above), and union leaders have (typically) opposed government rather than co-operated with it. The ability of national union leaders to provide effective leadership is doubtful because the national unions' financial weakness and the de-centralised nature of collective bargaining leave the union leader unable (in many cases) to offer any incentive to his members for their loyalty, nor has he effective power to discipline them.

The uniqueness of the U.K. labour movement is apparent. It is, moreover, linked to a strong proletarian spirit and belief in solidarity in action (indicated by high union membership).

Belgium, France, Italy and Britain show marked divisions of class. People in these countries have a sense of belonging to one class, and of not belonging to another. This causes basic antagonism in society. Denmark, Germany, the Netherlands and Norway, in contrast, are observed to have a stronger sense of national unity and of the importance of co-operation within the country.

In Britain, unlike France, Italy and Belgium, there is little scope for this proletarian spirit to be dissipated in viable political alternatives. In these continental European countries there are very strong political divisions – Conservative, Socialist and Communist – each well organised and exhibiting considerable animosity towards the others. Denmark, Germany, Norway and the United Kingdom are characterised by the absence of such basic splits. Differences in politics and the labour movement are of degree rather than kind, and there is an absence of religious animosity. In the United Kingdom therefore the proletarian spirit is unable to dissipate itself in viable alternative political activities, and neither is it concentrated and positively directed by a strongly centralised union movement able effectively to co-operate with and influence government. It is quite possible that this unique combination of factors has affected the rate of productivity growth in Britain.

How can labour reduce productivity growth? Possible ways include: insistence on over-manning (i.e. non-optimal capital: labour ratio), insisting on the retention of old practices (e.g. on non-optimal investment programmes), insisting on demarcation, insisting on labour – using status symbols (e.g. craftsmens' mates), restricting entry to certain trades (e.g. by artificially prolonged apprenticeship schemes), restricting output and by co-operating in collective bargaining techniques which protect inefficient firms. The greatest difficulty in judging the extent to which labour either aims at or succeeds in reducing productivity growth in these ways is in recognising what portion of blame lies with management rather than with labour. Management is, after all, the instigator and its quality in the United Kingdom has (as noted in Chapter 7) been adversely compared with that in other Western countries. A 1967 study of British industry by British executives of high rank did conclude that over-manning in much of U.K. industry stemmed more from managerial weakness than union restrictiveness [21]. Another study was also highly critical of large segments of British management [44]. On the other hand studies of shop stewards in action have indicated that they do play a powerful role in stopping spontaneous strikes, in sorting out workers' grievances, and in maintaining production, see, for example, Turner, Glack and Roberts [57].

Examination of the U.K. labour movement, and its comparison with those of other Western countries, suggests two major factors which may have contributed to Britain's relatively low productivity growth. These have been remarked upon above. The first is the nature of British society. It is still very class-conscious with considerable solidarity within classes and animosity between classes. This has led to a lack of co-operation between government and the labour movement which has been fostered on both sides. The second is the two-tier nature of the union organisation. This has left central union organisations relatively weak in relation to their members, and also in relation to the government. The union leader has only got very limited ability to lead, as noted above, and is left in a position of weakness *vis-à-vis* the government because of this. He is unable to strike a bargain with the national government because he has little to offer the government in exchange for concessions it might make to the unions. This has served to reinforce and perpetuate the first difficulty. The worker can still observe the 'us' and 'them' in society; in the United Kingdom (unlike all other Western countries with a highly unionised labour force) the unions do not play a direct role in governing the country.

This book is concerned with explanations of Britain's low rate of growth, not with prescriptions for increasing it. However, one must note that the difficulties of overcoming the two factors noted above are immense. No British government is likely to take over and reform the unions (as the Industrial Re-organisation Corporation has sought to do with firms). The weakness of the national unions *vis-à-vis* their lower tier is likely to make internal reform difficult or unwanted. Yet, if no such reform occurs, present divisions in U.K. society are likely to be perpetuated. The unions will not be able to participate effectively in formulating and managing a coherent national strategy for economic growth (or anything else) until they have centralised their activities and their power.

Alternative hopes that either affluence or education will overcome class prejudices seem ill-founded. A recent thorough study of affluent workers concluded:

> 'specifically middle class social norms are not widely followed nor life styles consciously emulated'
>
> and
>
> 'assimilation into middle class society is neither in process nor, in the main, a desired objective' [17].

Education, on the other hand, can only influence matters over a lengthy period of time.

9 Conclusion

It seems that there is no simple, straightforward economic explanation for the United Kingdom's low growth rate since the mid-1950s. The economic system is a complex *social* phenomenon, and its growth reflects the social, institutional and political factors which underlie the shallower economic transactions summarised in measures of gross national product and output. There is wide agreement amongst economists that increasing factor productivity is much more important in explaining growth than increases in factor input quantities. There is also widespread agreement that the continental European countries have been able to sustain high rates of economic growth over the last twenty years because they were able to redeploy labour away from low productivity (and even peasant) agriculture. Economic analysis is unable however to explain the generation of 'technical progress' (i.e. increasing factor productivity), or to show why the observed redeployment of labour occurred. Examination of the economic factors repeatedly points to the need for consideration of the social, political and institutional factors, and it is clear that the serious student of economic growth needs a broad knowledge of non-economic matters too.

As illustrated in Chapters 7 and 8, those who have studied economic growth patterns in the Western world are very aware of the need to include less straightforward economic arguments in their analysis. It is necessary to consider difficult questions about the quality of management, the nature of the labour force, the framework of collective bargaining, and underlying social and institutional factors, etc. in order to explain satisfactorily these patterns. Difficult as they may be these questions have to be faced; and their existence only adds to the fascination to be found in the study of growth. This book is no more than an introduction to such study.

Bibliography

[1] A. G. Armstrong and A. Silberston, 'Size of Plant, Size of Enterprise and Concentration in British Manufacturing Industry 1935–58', *Journal of the Royal Statistical Society*, Series A (1965).

[2] J. S. Bain, *International Differences in Industrial Structures, 8 Nations in the 1950's* (New Haven, Conn.: Yale University Press, 1966).

[3] C. Balfour, *Industrial Relations in the Common Market* (Routledge & Kegan Paul, 1973).

[4] T. Barna, *Investment and Growth Policies in British Industrial Firms* (Cambridge University Press, 1962).

[5] W. Beckerman, *et al.*, *The British Economy in 1975* (Cambridge University Press, 1965).

[6] R. E. Caves (ed.), *Britain's Economic Prospects* (Washington, D.C.: Brookings Institution; and Allen & Unwin, 1968).

[7] M. H. Cooper and J. E. S. Parker, 'Profitability and Foreign Owned Subsidiaries', *Business Ratios*, No. 3 (Autumn 1967).

[8] P. Deane and W. A. Cole, *British Economic Growth 1688–1959*, 2nd ed. (Cambridge University Press, 1969).

[9] E. F. Denison (assisted by J-P. Poulier), *Why Growth Rates Differ – Postwar Experience in Nine Western Countries.* (Washington, D.C.: Brookings Institution; and Allen & Unwin, 1967).

[10] E. F. Denison, 'Economic Growth', in *Britain's Economic Prospects*, ed. R. E. Caves (Washington, D.C.: Brookings Institution; and Allen & Unwin, 1968).

[11] J. C. R. Dow, *The Management of the British Economy, 1945–60* (Cambridge University Press, 1970).

[12] J. H. Dunning, 'U.S. Subsidiaries in Britain and their U.K. Competitors', *Business Ratios*, No. 1 (Autumn 1966).

[13] P. S. Florence, *The Logic of British and American Industry* (Routledge & Kegan Paul, 1972).

[14] M. Fores, 'Britain's Economic Growth and the 1870 Watershed', *Lloyds Bank Review* (January 1971).

[15] G. Freeman and A. Young, *The Research and Development Effort in Western Europe, North America and the Soviet Union* (Paris: O.E.C.D., 1965).
[16] Lord Fulton, *The Civil Service* (H.M.S.O., 1968).
[17] J. H. Goldthorpe and D. Lockwood, *The Affluent Worker in the Class Structure* (Cambridge University Press, 1971).
[18] D. Granick, *The European Executive* (New York: Doubleday, 1964).
[19] D. Hamberg, *Models of Economic Growth* (New York: Harper & Row, 1971).
[20] D. F. Heathfield, *Production Functions* (Macmillan Studies in Economics, Macmillan, 1972).
[21] H.M.S.O., *Efficient Use of Manpower* (Ministry of Labour, 1967).
[22] H.M.S.O., *Royal Commission on Trade Unions and Employers' Associations* (1966).
[23] E. J. Hobsbawm, *Industry and Empire* (Pelican, 1969).
[24] R. Hyman, *Strikes* (Fontana, 1972).
[25] M. D. Intriligator, 'Embodied Technical Change and Productivity in the U.S.A.', *Review of Economics and Statistics*, vol. 49 (February 1965).
[26] D. Jorgensen and Z. Griliches, 'The Explanation of Productivity Change', *Review of Economic Studies* (July 1967). Reprinted in [48].
[27] N. Kaldor, *Causes of the Slow Rate of Economic Growth of the United Kingdom* (Cambridge University Press, 1966).
[28] C. Kennedy and A. P. Thirlwall, 'Surveys in Applied Economics: Technical Progress', *Economic Journal* (March 1972).
[29] J. Knapp and K. Lomax, 'Britain's Growth Performance: Enigma of the 50's', *Lloyds Bank Review* (October 1964).
[30] J. A. Kregel, *The Theory of Economic Growth* (Macmillan Studies in Economics, Macmillan, 1972).
[31] S. Kuznets, 'The Economic Growth of Nations: Long Term Trends in Capital Formation Proportions', *Economic Development and Cultural Change* (July 1961).
[32] D. S. Landes, *The Unbound Prometheus* (Cambridge University Press, 1969).
[33] I. M. D. Little, *Critique of Welfare Economics*, 2nd ed. (Oxford University Press, 1957).
[34] A. Maddison, 'Explaining Economic Growth', *Banco Nazionale del Lavoro* (September 1972).
[35] W. E. J. McCarthy, 'The Role of Shop Stewards in British

Industrial Relations', *Royal Commission on Trade Unions and Employers' Associations Research Paper* (H.M.S.O., 1966).

[36] D. N. McCloskey (ed.), *Essays on a Mature Economy, Britain after 1840* (Methuen, 1971).

[37] N.E.D.O., *Investment Appraisal* (H.M.S.O., 1969).

[38] O.E.C.D., *Main Economic Indicators* (Paris, 1970).

[39] O.E.C.D., *The Growth of Output 1960–80* (Paris, 1970).

[40] O.E.C.D., *The Outlook for Economic Growth* (Paris, 1970).

[41] O.E.C.D., *National Accounts 1950–1969* (Paris, 1971).

[42] O.E.C.D., *The Overall Level and Structure of Research and Development Efforts in Member Countries* (Paris, 1967).

[43] M. J. Peck, 'Science and Technology', in *Britain's Economic Prospects*, ed. R. E. Caves [6].

[44] P.E.P., *Attitudes in British Management* (Pelican, 1966).

[45] M. Postan, *Economic History of Western Europe 1945–64* (Methuen, 1967).

[46] C. Pratten, R. M. Dean and A. Silberston, *The Economics of Large Scale Production in British Industry* (Cambridge University Press, 1965).

[47] P. A. Samuelson, 'Evaluation of Real National Income', *Oxford Economic Papers* (1950).

[48] A. K. Sen (ed.), *Growth Economics* (Penguin, 1970).

[49] M. Shanks, *The Stagnant Society* (Pelican, 1972).

[50] W. G. Shepherd, 'Industrial Concentration in the U.S.A. and Britain', *Review of Economics and Statistics* (February 1961).

[51] W. G. Shepherd, 'Changes in British Industrial Concentration 1951–58', *Oxford Economic Papers* (March 1966)

[52] R. M. Solow, 'Technical Change and the Aggregate Production Function', *Review of Economics and Statistics*, vol. 39 (1957). Reprinted in [48].

[53] R. M. Solow, *Growth Theory* (Oxford University Press, 1969).

[54] R. M. Solow, 'Technical Progress, Capital Formation and Economic Growth', *American Economic Association Papers* (May 1962).

[55] R. M. Solow, *Capital Theory and the Rate of Return* (North-Holland, 1963).

[56] W. A. Turner, *Is Britain Really Strike Prone?* (Cambridge University Press, 1969).

[57] W. A. Turner, G. Glack and G. Roberts, *Labour Relations in the Motor Industry* (Allen & Unwin, 1967).

[58] L. Ulman, 'Collective Bargaining and Industrial Efficiency', in *Britain's Economic Prospects*, ed. R. E. Caves [6].

...s Bank

...ractice